Gospel
Days

Gospel Days

Reflections for Every Day of the Year

Joan Chittister

ORBIS BOOKS

Maryknoll, New York 10545

Photo credits:
  Joe Vail: pp. 8 and 92
  Megan McKenna: pp. 28, 40, 80, 105, 126, and 138
  John Beeching, M.M.: pp. 16 and 53
  J. Padula: p. 116
  A. F. Sozio from Gendreau: p. 150

The Catholic Foreign Mission Society of America (Maryknoll) recruits and trains people for overseas missionary service. Through Orbis Books, Maryknoll aims to foster the international dialogue that is essential to mission. The books published, however, reflect the opinions of their authors and are not meant to represent the official position of the society. To obtain more information about Maryknoll or Orbis Books, please visit our website at http://www.maryknoll.org.

Originally published as *The Monastic Way 1998* by BENETVISION, Erie, PA 16503

Copyright © 1999 Joan D. Chittister

Published by Orbis Books, Maryknoll, New York, U.S.A.

Manufactured in the United States of America

Library of Congress Cataloging-in-Publication Data

Chittister, Joan.
    Gospel days : reflections for every day of the year / Joan
Chittister.
       p. cm.
    ISBN 1-57075-280-X (pbk.)
    1. Bible. N.T. Gospels Meditations. 2. Devotional calendars.
I. Title.
BS2555.4 .C47   1999
242'.2 – dc21   99-31687

*This book is dedicated to the women of all time
whose spiritual wisdom was never noted, never collected,
never made available to the rest of the world.*

Introduction

At one point or another in life, we all hear the gospels. And at one level or another, we all ignore them. Either we dismiss them as meaningless and so reject them or we dismiss them as revered but belonging to another world, not ours. Both positions are, at best, unfortunate. The gospels changed the face of human belief and so can surely change us, too. That's not meaningless. Our world is still nourished by them. That's not irrelevant.

This is a book about the gospel life now and here, about its daily demands and common questions. Most of all, it is about the way the gospels call us to respond to life. Finally, it is a simple demonstration of the enduring model of a monastic spirituality that is over fifteen hundred years old.

Monastic spirituality immerses a person in the scriptures. Monastic communities, in fact, read the scriptures at least three times a day and, in many places, also read as part of these same public prayer periods various commentaries on those scriptures that

emerge from the earliest centuries of the church. Such continuing reminders of the way the Christian community interpreted those scriptures over time is an esteemed and valuable process. It brings forward for the ages the classical sense of every passage. But, in the end, what really counts is what those scriptures say to us. Now. About our own lives in our own time.

Monastic spirituality calls this process of personal reflection on scripture *lectio*. This thoughtful reading of a scripture passage — a scene, a sentence, a word — and its challenge to present circumstances and private choices is the foundation of a faith rooted in the spirit of Jesus. It brings to the bar of the gospel my own life.

This book is the product of my own *lectio* over the years. My hope is that it will prompt your reading of scripture, too — with fresh eyes and a new heart. The question to which *lectio* must always bring us, my formation director said, is: What is this passage saying to me, demanding of me, calling out to me today? And she was right. This approach to scripture has challenged my soul for years, sometimes strengthening it, always stretching it.

My hope is that this book will begin your own dialogue with the scriptures. I promise you new life for the effort.

JOAN CHITTISTER, O.S.B.

9

We read the same parts of scripture so many times that as the years go by we often fail to hear them at all. Here we will concentrate on some of those familiar passages and ask what those words might mean to us now. Recite the line from scripture every day and let it seep into your soul.

JANUARY

LUKE 6:45

*A good person
produces good
from the good treasure
of the heart.*

Martin Luther King Jr. defied the government for the sake of desegregation. Dorothy Day was arrested for insisting on women's suffrage. Thousands of American boys refused to fight an undeclared war in Vietnam. Whites sold property to blacks in "white" neighborhoods when the neighborhood didn't want it. Whole segments of the society considered those things wrong to do. So who was right? And what is goodness? And how do we know?

Jesus says in Luke that it all depends on what's in the heart when we do those things. It's why we do what we do that counts. But there's the stumbling block. Why we do anything is hardly ever for a single reason. Our motives aren't just mixed; they are often in contradiction to one another.

The heart is not an arrow. It is an amalgam of magnets all pulling in different directions. It is commitment to family, commitment to self, commitment to success, commitment to life, commitment to God, commitment to security, commitment to approval all jangled and knotted and demanding. Goodness is the ability to choose one over the other when it counts.

And when does it really count? It counts when someone else's life will suffer if we do not muster the courage to make the right choice in this situation at this time in this place.

"Those who have lived well in their own time have lived well for all time," the ancients say. It's the choices we make today that determine the character of tomorrow in this country. And most essential of all, perhaps, to the nature of goodness is the fact that not to choose — not to get involved, not to decide, not to bother — is the most serious choice of all.

January 1: Goodness is not rule-keeping; it is right-doing for right reasons. We so often do things because we feel we cannot do otherwise and still become as socially acceptable as we would like to be. So we give to charities or sign petitions or join committees or volunteer at social events. Each action is surely a good thing. Whether or not it is "goodness" is another discussion.

January 2: Nothing is more boring than social "goodness." Nothing is more exciting than moral goodness. It's when we do what must be done, whatever the cost, that life reaches its highest pitch.

January 3: Elizabeth Barrett Browning wrote:

> *We all have known*
> *Good critics, who have stamped out poet's hopes;*
> *Good statesmen, who pulled ruin on the state;*
> *Good patriots, who, for a theory, risked a cause;*
> *Good kings, who disemboweled for a tax;*
> *Good Popes, who brought all good to jeopardy;*
> *Good Christians, who sat still in easy chairs;*
> *And damned the general world for standing up. —*
> *Now, may the good God pardon all good men!*

Point: Beware the kind of goodness that destroys anything in the name of superior virtue.

January 4: Goodness, scripture is clear, is not determined by good deeds but by the quality of goodness that reigns in our hearts.

January 5: So much evil is done in the name of doing good. Jews were driven out of Spain for the sake of Christianity. Noncombatant Japanese were exterminated for the sake of saving soldiers in World War II. Babies go hungry when we force their parents to find work that does not pay enough to feed them. What do we do about goodness like that?

January 6: It is so easy to criticize people for not being good enough when we have no idea how bad they could be if they weren't as good as they are.

January 7: Goodness is a virtue, not a "role." The good mother, the good sister, the good woman makes a person a thing. What we really need are women who can function out of their hearts, not out of the public expectations and definitions imposed on them by others. Sometimes breaking a role to find a person is the greatest good we can do.

January 8: George Orwell wrote, "On the whole, human beings want to be good, but not too good, and not quite all the time." And that sounds very healthy to me. The "good" child who lives up to everyone else's expectations all the time is too often a time bomb waiting to happen. Life is an exploration, not a straightjacket. Goodness is what I do because it must be done, not what I do because I have no other choice.

January 9: The present Buddhist patriarch of Cambodia, Maha Ghosananda, saw his entire family killed by the Khmer Rouge. And he is the one who initiated the Walks for Peace through the Khmer Rouge countryside in the hope of bringing the country to reconciliation. Now that's goodness.

January 10: Everything we do in life, the scripture reminds us, goes into the treasury of the heart. The ideas with which we fill our hearts determine the way we live our lives. Those are the things we draw on in those moments when we need to reach down deep inside ourselves for character, courage, endurance, and hope. That's why what we read, what we see, and what we do from day to day counts so much in life.

January 11: "Good, the more communicated, more abundant grows," John Milton wrote. What we note and praise and affirm and publicize changes the world.

January 12: If we want to know how much good we do, we need to ask ourselves how much good we do for which we do not get paid. Good work and work that is good are two different things.

January 13: A Chinese proverb reads: "To talk goodness is not good — only to do it is." The question becomes: To what degree do we involve ourselves personally in making possible what we say is good?

January 14: Goodness is not a single act in a sea of indifference. It is a pattern of actions, a habit of acting that starts in principle and ends in courage.

January 15: To be smart is an accident, to be beautiful is a cultural definition, but to be good is a choice.

January 16: The thing that's wrong with goodness is that it too often masks as piety but lacks principle.

January 17: Goodness carries us through the hard moments of life and brings us out better on the other side. It is patience when we have reason to be frustrated, generosity when we qualify to be frugal, the public commitment to truth when not a soul in the world would be expecting us to speak out.

January 18: Making a moral mistake or becoming socially indifferent is not what makes a person bad. Badness is the point at which we cease to care what effect our own actions will have on others.

January 19: Ralph Waldo Emerson wrote: "The meaning of good and bad, of better and worse, is simply helping or hurting."

January 20: "If a friend is in trouble," Edgar Watson Howe wrote, "don't annoy them by asking if there is anything you can do. Think up something appropriate and do it." "Just call if you need something" is no gift at all, in other words. It is a false promise in an empty box.

January 21: This is the century in which we set out to irradiate not one city but two, both Hiroshima and Nagasaki; in which we invented the end of the world and stored it in the corn fields of Kansas; in which we put more money into weapons than into public welfare programs; in which science became religion; and in which technology, rather than ethics, became the norm of the doable. And we wonder why young people don't hold as good the values on which we were raised.

January 22: "No one can be good for long," Bertolt Brecht wrote, "if goodness is not in demand." What we expect in a society is what we will get. Very few people can live beyond the standards of the society in which they exist. Those who do are saints; those who don't are normal.

January 23: Lots of things seem to be goodness that are simply political choices. It's when we do what must be done despite the fact that people either won't understand or won't approve that the grain of goodness grows to fullness in us. Don't be discouraged. It is often a lifetime in coming.

January 24: Goodness grows in us like flowers grow in any garden: by being planted and watered and nourished.

January 25: Goodness is a process of becoming, not of being. What we do over and over again is what we become in the end. In the meantime, Agnes Repplier comforts us with this: "Our dogs will love and admire the meanest of us, and feed our colossal vanity with their uncritical homage."

January 26: Courage can be a hidden virtue. Faith can be personal. Goodness is the kind of character trait, however, that cannot be practiced alone. Goodness requires a public posture. To be good you have to be good to someone else. Makes you think, doesn't it?

January 27: We like to believe that there is a supernatural source of all evil. We refuse to admit, Joseph Conrad says, that we ourselves are quite capable of doing all the evil there is. Indeed, who of us has not already done it, at least in microcosm? But once we realize that, we are suddenly capable of the immeasurable good that comes from humility.

January 28: The love we owe our friends is a commitment to their own goodness. Those who enable us, justify us, in our weaknesses do not love us; they are exploiting us for some reason of their own.

January 29: Who we are today is what the future will be like. The future, you see, has already arrived. We are it — for good or ill.

January 30: Never confuse goodness and acceptability, goodness and conformity, goodness and piety. They are dangerous confusions.

January 31: What is goodness? It is the person in your life who surprised you with virtue at a time when evil would have been understandable.

FEBRUARY

LUKE 8:1–3

*The twelve disciples went with him,
and so did some women...
who used their own resources to help.*

When I was about thirteen years old, I made my first visit to New York City. I had one destination in mind: My heart was set on seeing the Empire State Building. I scanned every horizon and compared every building I could see with what I could remember of pictures in encyclopedias and grade school magazines; I watched every street sign for a clue to its location. The height of that building was the one piece of information about the Big City that had leaked into my little Pennsylvania school. It alone tied me to the town, gave me a grounding, confirmed the fact that small town U.S.A. was not hopelessly unconnected to the world at large. It was the one thing, I knew, that could achieve any degree whatsoever of a social balance of power between my New Jersey cousins and me. I had to spot it first or be branded hopelessly country. Survival demanded it.

So, while my mother and aunt went in and out of stores, I walked the streets of New York, head back, gawking at one building after another and calculating their heights. Finally, a little dizzy, my cousins and I stopped to lean against the nearest building. I shook my head out, stretched my neck and without any warning at all, suddenly saw the thing. "There it is!" I yelled to my cousin. "It's down there." I pointed at a building blocks beyond *us. "Oh, it is not," my cousin snapped back, older, superior. "That's it on the other corner." We took bets — she counting on her status as a local, I betting on a picture in an encyclopedia — and leaned back against the building again to look cool and disdainful while we waited for a referee to square things. "Aunt Helen," I demanded when our mothers came out of the store, "which one of us is right, Ellen or me? Is that the Empire State Building on the left side of that street down there or is it the building on the other corner?" "It's neither," she said. "You two are leaning against it."*

I learned that day how the obvious can be invisible. It was an invaluable lesson. I have since watched the world around me routinely obliterate reality and understand, as a result, how easily it can happen. And no one even knows they're doing it. I have decided, in fact, that the principle functions with special acuity where women are concerned. We don't, as a culture, a world, a church, see women. We see what we expect to see, what we're willing to see, what we're trained to see, what we define as significant. Everything else becomes invisible, becomes the furniture of life, becomes extraneous — like butlers and waitresses. Except, of course, in the gospels, where what is pointed out is what's really important. "And there were women and children in the crowd," the evangelist says. Unfortunately, they have seldom been noticed since.

YOUR ORDER IS AT CODYS BOOKS
BRING THIS CARD TO THE INFORMATION DESK

TITLE: GOSPEL DAYS
AUTHOR: CHITTISTER
QUANTITY: 1
ISBN/CODE: 157075280X
CATEGORY: SPE   PETER   2 MENARD-WARWICK
DATE: 05/18/00   300 GOODING WAY #321
DEPOSIT: 14.00
PRICE: 14.00   ALBANY   CA 94706
KK0240046   JOBSPO

0000155909 16
            PUB4   4TH ST

February 1: What a nation really values it raises monuments to, sculpts statues for, names buildings as, inscribes cornerstones to. We say repeatedly how much we value women. Take a piece of paper and write down all the statues, monuments, buildings, and cornerstones you have ever seen inscribed to a woman. The funny thing is that the evangelist names them right up front. How do we explain the difference?

February 2: The only philanthropists named in Jesus' life are women "who used their own resources to help," the gospel says. But philanthropists are people who see the value of what other people have yet to recognize and make sure it happens by supporting it themselves. No women, no Jesus, in other words. I'd call that a very important dimension of the ministry — or at least that's what people seem to think when they name buildings for the men who donated them. In which case, you can't help but wonder why is it we never see women as the builders of Jesus' ministry.

February 3: Jesus talked to women as equals — as he did with Mary Magdalene; taught women about theological issues — as he did with Mary of Bethany; and sent women to preach to others — as he did the Samaritan woman. When he did those things with men, they called themselves disciples. When he does it with women, it's called nothing at all.

February 4: Feminist spirituality points us toward a contemporary spirituality, a new worldview. Feminist spirituality asks both men and women to look at life from the bias of the beatitudes with hearts of flesh where hearts of stone once went unchallenged.

February 5: To feminists, a spirituality that does not release the feminine dimension in both women and men leaves all humanity half-souled, the church half-graced, and the world half-developed.

February 6: Feminism is not a women's question: It is the human question of the century. It is the spiritual question of all time. It's not about getting what men already have. Not on your life. What men have is not nearly enough. Feminism is about getting a better world for everybody.

February 7: Feminism does not destroy men. If anything, it comes to save men from an imprisonment by a system that cramps the human development of all men while it purports to give them power. Feminism comes to bring both men and women to the fullness of life and wholeness of soul for which we were all made "in the image and likeness of God."

February 8: If we are to take the scripture seriously, then, clearly, we are all surrounded by the presence of God in one another. And if we are all "words of God," then each of us, all of us, have something to say. We are all messages to the rest of the world of the nature and mind of God. We are all expressions of divine presence, of divine hope, of divine truth. We are all meant to be word to one another. And women, too, have a word to say about how this world is run which must be heard. We ignore it to our peril.

February 9: Feminism sees otherness as a way to enrich a society. Conference tables, conclaves, synods, parliaments, and bank boards that are all old, all white, all male, and all middle-class may have power but they lack perspective because they lack complexity. They lack a sense of what they do not know.

February 10: Feminist spirituality follows the Jesus who sought out tax collectors and zealots, women and children, Pharisees and paralytics pronounced to be in sin and raised them all to the full height of their souls, and of his. Respect for otherness is a basic component of a feminist worldview.

February 11: As long as a woman is required to be less than she should be, a man will be required to be more than he can be — and to the detriment of both of them.

February 12: The best thing that happens to a woman is when she discovers that she too is a full human being with abilities, gifts, and dreams. The worst thing that happens to a woman is when she discovers that she too is a full human being with abilities, gifts, and dreams.

February 13: "My love for an institution," the philosopher John Stuart Mill wrote, "is in proportion to my desire to reform it." The desire to have it recognized that "there were women in the crowd" is not a desire to destroy the system; it is the desire to bring it to fullness.

February 14: Feminists come in two genders: male as well as female. How do we know? Because "feminism" is simply a commitment to the full humanity, total dignity, and unrestricted equality of opportunity for all human beings, regardless of sex, despite social gender roles.

February 15: When we say "masculine" we think "strong." When we say "feminine" we think "weak." When we say "feminist" we think "aggressive." What a sad commentary on a limited view of life.

February 16: I know, I know: "Jesus didn't ordain a woman." But the fact is that Jesus didn't ordain anybody. He wouldn't have dreamed of it in a culture where "priesthood" was an inherited position reserved for members of the tribe of Levi — none of whom, apparently, were apostles. Jesus didn't have "priests." He had "apostles" and "disciples" and "women who ministered to him." But since then, women haven't been able to minister to anyone. Officially. That sounds like a long way from Galilee to me.

February 17: The wag said: "Ginger Rogers did everything that Fred Astaire did. She just did it backwards and in high heels." What else is new?

February 18: Whoever decided that women are "inherently passive and peaceful" didn't know Margaret Thatcher. Whoever decided that women are less intelligent than men didn't know Madame Curie. Whoever decided that women are essentially weaker than men didn't know anything about actuarial tables. The fact is simply that women aren't essentially anything but human. It's time to start living like that so that "the war between the sexes" can become the partnership between the sexes.

February 19: The contention of some is that men are superior to women because Genesis says that a man was created first. Not a single word about the animals who were created before the man. So much for the primacy argument.

February 20: It isn't femaleness that counts, it's feminism — those qualities in both women and men that make feeling, compassion, heart, and service as important as reason, strength, law, and power.

February 21: We talk a lot about mothering when it is parenting that counts. Interestingly enough, children with active fathers — fathers who feed, dress, wash, entertain, and talk to them — score higher on both academic and social indicators than children with fathers who are distant. The point is clear: Rigid role definitions hurt our children as well as ourselves.

February 22: Men suffer from sexism, too. They are taught as very young children not to cry, not to feel, not to fail, not to show weakness. They're told to work harder, earn more, get ahead, make money.

And they drop dead trying to do it all. Sexism renders women invisible, yes, but it kills men. Literally.

February 23: "A holy person," the proverb says, "is someone in whose presence I feel sacred about myself." Those who diminish the other simply reveal the lack in themselves.

February 24: They were loud, they went to jail, they were dismissed by "good" women, they were denounced by ministers, they were force fed by policemen. They weren't "nice." They were your grandmothers. They were suffragettes. And they were right.

February 25: No one in Jesus' time noticed women. So why did the evangelists write about them? Because, it was clear, they were as involved as men in the ministry of Jesus, and Jesus thought they were important and wanted us to think the same. Clearly, that part of the gospel is still to be fulfilled in us.

February 26: To make invisible is the art of ignoring what we do not want to see because it stands to make demands on us. What conversion is necessary, I wonder, before women are no longer the invisible ones of the world. And whose?

February 27: World Watch Institute tells us that of the 8,000 abortions performed in Bombay after amniocentesis several years ago, 7,999 of them were of female fetuses. That is not abortion. That is female infanticide. The question is, "What is it in society that could possibly fuel such a slaughter and why?"

February 28: It was the prophetess Anna, not Simeon, who announced the birth of Jesus, the greatest proclamation of all time, to the people in the Temple. Look it up. Imagine what the world would be like if there had been as many women as men developing the political documents and theological statements upon which societies everywhere have been built.

MARCH

MARK 8:25

Jesus placed his hands
on the man's eyes.
This time he saw
everything clearly.

Y ou can't absolve the Irish," the old joke goes: "They feel guilty for everything and sorry for nothing." It took me years to understand the implications of the remark, but I finally got the point. Confession, penance, atonement all have to do with wrongdoing, not with wrong thinking. There's a message there for all of us, perhaps. There's a difference between good guilt and bad guilt, between real guilt and false guilt. To grow as human beings, we need to be able to tell one from the other.

Guilt has gone out of fashion in the Western world. That's a shame. So much good comes out of guilt. Without it, what would ever drive us to change our lives for the better when we find ourselves losing our grip on conscience and conviction. We so often focus more on either denial or punishment than we do on the vision and the wisdom that can come out of recognizing our weaknesses and rededicating our lives to the values we hold and the ideals we seek.

This society is much more inclined, it seems, to talk about personal "growth" than about personal "guilt," more about strategies for self-promotion than about the development of inner vision. And the imbalance shows, both in the moral chaos that marks our social system and in the *lack of moral limits that results from our almost fanatical pursuit of self-development in a highly individualistic culture. It's not difficult to understand what spawned the situation, of course. Disdainful of one extreme we have developed another and lost some of the most important spiritual wisdom in the lexicon of the human race as a result.*

A highly religious culture with roots in Jansenism and Puritanism, we experienced the fear and self-loathing that comes out of hell-and-damnation sermons, darkly inflated concentration on human sinfulness, and the loss of a sense of natural human goodness. To combat such negative and exaggerated disdain of the human condition we created an environment that confuses the moral, the immoral, and the amoral. Now few people feel guilty about anything. It may be time to rediscover the glory of guilt and the mental and spiritual health that can come from it. Or is the notion of human responsibility a myth?

40

March 1: The fourteenth-century English mystic Julian of Norwich taught that sin "is behoovable but that all shall be well." Sin is good for us, in other words, if we learn something about ourselves that leads us to become more mature than we were before it happened. It's called "learning the hard way" but it can, if we let it, be learning, nevertheless.

March 2: The things that bother my conscience are telling me something about the difference between what I am and what I want to be. It pays to listen to the small voice deep within. As Barbara Mraz says, "Guilt is an emotion that has periodically served me well."

March 3: Guilt is the spiritual vision that enables me to keep myself and all of life in perspective. In Jesus' time, sickness was thought to be God's punishment for sin. When Jesus, in defiance of public opinion, gives sight to the blind man rather than leave him to what was seen as God's eternal punishment, it was a call to everybody to see sin differently. We are all called at some time in life to do the same.

March 4: Once I have felt guilt, I become a softer part of the human race. I am, then, prepared to be far more kind to other people who have also failed their own best aspirations than I could ever be to them without it.

March 5: Shame is the caution light of the heart. It stops us from giving ourselves over to what we do not want to become but now realize we are more than capable of being.

March 6: Guilt protects us from those impulses within us which are less to be feared than they are to be understood.

March 7: Those who have never known guilt have never known their own best selves.

March 8: "Oh, happy fault," the church sings in the Easter liturgy. Without the crucifixion, in other words, no resurrection. The message is painfully clear. Sometimes, without great sin, we get no great insights either.

March 9: Healthy guilt is neither scrupulosity nor rationalization. It does not make something out of nothing, nor does it make nothing out of something. It simply looks personal failure in the eye and says, "I can do better than that."

March 10: The nice thing about guilt is that it proves that we are still alive. If we can still feel moral angst, we can feel everything else in life, too.

March 11: "Rabbi," the disciples said, "why do you teach that God is closer to sinners than to the perfect ones?" "Well," the old rabbi explained, "every time we sin, we break the thread that ties us to God. Every time we repent, God ties it up again. And every knot shortens the thread." Now, isn't that a lovely thought? It is the weakness of the soul that brings us always closer to God, not its perfectionism.

March 12: The first sign of healthy guilt is that we never feel guilty for the wrong things. Guilt always has something to do with failing to recognize my creaturehood or hurting someone else. Think of the ten commandments: The first three have to do with recognizing that God is God and not making ourselves the center of the universe; the next seven have to do with doing harm to others. As in "Love God; love the other." Simple. Nothing else counts. Not really. The question that measures guilt is always: Who was harmed?

March 13: The second sign of healthy guilt is that it is not exaggerated. Spiritual vision is the ability to see things as they are. Some of our struggles are serious; some of them are not. Some of our moral arm wrestling matches of life are long-standing and need to be uprooted; some of them are only momentary breakdowns in an otherwise well-ordered soul.

March 14: Some of the moral decision-making moments of our lives revolve around things we regularly find difficult to cope with. They are the recurring struggles of our life, and the way we deal with them will, in the end, define our character. These things we too often ignore. Some of them are simply symptoms of the tension of the day. These things we too often agonize over. Look at all of them closely and give each of them the amount of attention they deserve. And no more.

March 15: Exaggerated guilt is called neurosis. On the other hand, exaggerated guiltlessness is neurotic, too. Both of those positions are out of touch with reality.

March 16: The third sign of healthy guilt is that we do something about it and put the situation behind us. The purpose of guilt always is simply to enable us to recognize the pitfalls of the present so that we can do better the next time, not to wallow in the past.

March 17: Never to feel guilty for anything I've done is to be a spiritual child. Always to feel guilty for things without substance is to be a spiritual invalid.

March 18: Life is not about its end point. It is about the journey, about the way we're getting where we're going. Those moments of realization which we call guilt can change the course of that life for the better.

March 19: The opposite of guilt is not righteousness; it is the vision we have acquired to see the purpose of struggle in life. Struggle is what leads us to clarify values and make knowledgeable choices.

March 20: It not only takes vision to see beyond someone else's weaknesses but it takes vision to be able to see beyond our own. Struggles keep us in touch with our own humanity and the humanity of those around us. My mother said once, in the face of great arrogance, "What that man needs is one good mortal sin." Between her and Julian of Norwich, I got the message: Sin is not a prescription but it is often a cure.

March 21: Spiritual maturity has to do with the ability to see life and ourselves for what we are. When we begin to realize our needs and where they come from within us, we can begin to satisfy those needs in ways that are not destructive of anyone, including ourselves.

March 22: "Guilt is the one burden," Anaïs Nin writes, "that human beings can't bear alone." Talking to someone else when we have disappointed ourselves is key to being able to get a perspective on the events. What we do in the throes of emotional pressure measures only the moment, not the essential quality of character. Growth is just that: It is a process.

March 23: "What do you do in the monastery," the visitor asked the monk. "Oh, we fall and we get up and we fall and we get up and we fall and we get up," the monk answered thoughtfully. And don't we all. The defining step in the spiritual life is simply the ability to admit it.

March 24: It is only when we fail to routinely examine the integrity of what we do that we have really stopped being honorable.

March 25: Guilt is not a matter of failing to meet the standards set by others. It involves the failures we suffer in keeping the standards we set for ourselves. If this society lacks guilt, it may be more that we lack values than that we lack conscience. The problem is not that we're bad people. The problem is that we no longer agree on what to be good about.

March 26: God does not want us to be trapped by guilt. God wants us to be freed by it to make new judgments, to evaluate our lives, to rise another step on the ladder of the self.

March 27: Healthy guilt is not simply the fear of getting caught. That's just "fear of getting caught." Healthy guilt is knowing that there is something in us that is crying out to be ameliorated.

March 28: When we follow the life of Jesus, the laws he broke and why, we begin to see what is really important. That's what saves us from a kind of guilt that is either sick or superficial. Then we become concerned about the really big things in life: the outcasts of society, the poor, the children, the handicapped, the women, and the good of the other. If we ever developed a sense of guilt about those things, we would have a completely different world.

March 29: We must begin to see what we are, who we are, what we have. That's the beginning of real spiritual insight. How we get all these things, how we use them and develop the conscience to feel guilty about abusing any of them is the baseline of moral evaluation.

March 30: R. D. Laing wrote, "True guilt is guilt at the obligation one owes to oneself to be oneself. False guilt is guilt felt at not being what other people feel one ought to be or assume that one is."

March 31: Real guilt is a process. Or as the wag wrote:

> *King Solomon and King David led very merry lives*
> *with very many concubines and very many wives*
> *until old age came creeping with very many qualms.*
> *Then Solomon wrote the proverbs and David wrote*
> *the psalms.*

Don't give up. Guilt, the grace of regret, is often what comes long after the action is done.

APRIL

MARK 1:35

*Jesus went out
to a lonely place,
where he prayed.*

The flight from Manila to Tokyo had been, to all appearances, totally routine. We were about an hour from touchdown when the captain came on the intercom: "When we left Manila," the voice said, "we got a signal from the on-board computer telling us that there is something wrong with the plane's landing gear. We have no idea what that is or how serious it may be. Your cabin crew will instruct you how to prepare for a crash landing. Emergency vehicles will meet us on the runway. Please listen carefully now to your flight attendant...." The schoolboy next to me said, "How do I tell them to call my sister first? I don't want my mother to hear about this on a phone." Then the noise in the cabin stopped. The entire planeload of tourists and business people, of whole families and solitary travelers like me went dead, cold, silent. For almost an hour we packed up our gear, removed glasses and shoes and jewelry. Then we simply sat and waited, frozen in silence through the sharp descent, the screeching down the runway, the final, sudden, lurching, landing amid the field of waiting ambulances and fire trucks that, in the end, were never needed. "Did you say a prayer?" someone asked me later when, home, safe, and long out of danger, I was telling the story. "No," I said. "I didn't say a prayer; I became a prayer."

Prayer comes on many levels, in many shapes, and at many moments in life. None of them are really predictable. All of them are real.

There are books aplenty written on the subject of prayer, of course, but I have come to the point where I doubt that anybody can really "teach" anybody how to pray. That, I figure, is what life does. We can learn prayer forms, of course, but we do not learn either the function or the purpose of prayer until life drags us to it, naked and in pain.

Theologians of the late nineteenth and early twentieth centuries were very good at dissecting prayer. There was spoken prayer, silent prayer, prayer of the mind, prayer of the heart and union with God, they told us. And approximately in that order, if I remember correctly all the manuals I read on the subject. It all seems pretty amusing to me now. I was trying to learn to pray exactly the same way I learned to run a printing press. By the book. In both cases I discovered that the only way to learn to do it was to do it for a long, long time.

They also taught us that there were four purposes of prayer: "adoration, contrition, thanksgiving, and supplication." Now there was something useful. Boring for years, not at all inspiring, perhaps, but more and more useful as life went on, not because it said much about prayer, but because it said so much about life.

Most important of all though, at least for me, was the line in the Rule of Benedict that instructs the monas-

tic community to keep prayer brief and the monastics to leave chapel quietly so that anybody who wants to stay behind for private prayer can do so without interruption. In those two simple statements I learned enough about prayer to last me for a lifetime: First, that in order to learn to pray we need to do it regularly. And second, that real contemplative prayer starts where formal prayer ends.

Point: Prayer is not a "technique." It is an attitude of mind, a quality of soul, and a dimension of the daily.

April 1: Prayer erupts in the heart at the sight of either the impossibly beautiful or the unbearably difficult. It is, in both cases, a signal of the breakthrough of the divine into the mundane.

April 2: Prayer is an attitude toward life that sees everything as ultimately sacred, everything as potentially life-changing, everything as revelatory of life's meaning. It is our link between dailiness and eternity.

April 3: Prayer is an admission of creaturehood. There is, we acknowledge when we pray, something greater than us in the universe, something more important than ourselves, something that holds everything together and makes it meaningful. And it is in the end benevolent. Do we understand it? No. Do we see it at work in life? Without a doubt.

April 4: Short prayers at stoplights, as in "Dear Jesus, please make the light turn green," are not prayers at all, of course, but they do what prayer is meant to do: They "raise our minds and hearts to God," who smiles on us just the same — when the light turns green.

April 5: We think of prayer as formal prayers, the kind we said as children. And no one should discount the value of those ready-made messages and pleadings. They root the thought of the presence of God very deeply in our souls. They create a treasure house of spiritual concepts that emerge in later life to steer us through both joy and tragedy. And yet prayer is far more than formal prayers. It is most of all the turning over of our lives to God. It is an affirmation of holy trust.

April 6: We do not pray prayers to coax God to save us from ourselves. The fights we start we are more than capable of ending. The weapons we make we ourselves can destroy. The jobs we get or lose we can learn from. No, we do not pray to change God. We pray so that God can change us. Those who pray prepare for the in-breaking of God in their lives.

April 7: For prayer to bring strength when we need it, we must pray regularly, even when we think we don't need it at all. Prayer is a habit of life that leads us to reflection, to consciousness of God, to the hope that is the lighthouse of the soul guiding us always through all the dark places of life.

April 8: Prayer is not a magic act; it is a relationship that calls the spiritual dimension in us to life, that attunes us to the universe, that hears the sound of the great "I Am" everywhere.

April 9: Supplication reveals the heart, admits our dependence, confesses our helplessness, and gives us the opportunity to accept life as it is rather than insist that life be lived on our terms only. When we lack something and turn to God for it, we may not find what we think we lack but we will definitely find what we need.

April 10: Contrition drains the soul of the dregs of life. It throws itself on the mercy of a God who, having flung us and this world into existence, loves us no matter what, understands that growth so often comes only through error and, seeing the direction of our hearts, thinks nothing of our mistakes. Contrition is the prayer that says "I love you; forgive me." And those who love us always do.

April 11: Thanksgiving is the dimension of prayer that allows gratitude to break through fear, confusion, uncertainty, and despair with trust. Thanksgiving says — in the face of either great gifts or great challenges — that with God's help we can survive both.

April 12: Adoration, one of the purposes of prayer, comes at that moment in time when we recognize the beauty of life, the graces of our own life — whatever its difficulties — the awesomeness of the universe, and the certainty that underneath it all lies a mystery beyond us. True, everything in this world is not right. Some people live in relentless poverty, embarrassing tragedy, inhuman injustice. But in the center of us, we know it was not meant to be that way. And for that we can, whatever the present situation, sing alleluia.

April 13: Everyone needs a favorite prayer, the kind that rises to our lips when there are no other words in life that express our vacant, empty need and the best hopes of our heart. I have two: "The Memorare" and "The Prayer of St. Francis." What's yours?

April 14: Sometimes the best prayer comes out of reading rather than praying. Good reading touches all the questions of our life, stretches us beyond ourselves to find answers, and brings us face-to-face with the Mystery that is God. Benedictines call that *lectio.* Thoughtful reading. Prayerful reading. Reading designed to bring us into contact with the essentials of life. Reading that stirs the best in us.

April 15: All real prayer is, at its deepest point, silent. It is what goes on inside of us because of what we have come to understand through human experience about the human relationship with God.

April 16: God is not a vending machine. The purpose of prayer is not to secure a shaky future with a God who exists to tantalize a world with presents. The purpose of prayer is to create the kind of relationship with God that makes life bigger than it can ever be without the God who created us.

April 17: Jesus goes out to pray because he needed, as we do, to recognize the face of God in unlikely places. It is not that humanity is far from God. It is that God is hidden under human guises that it takes our entire lives to recognize. And then, only if we make a habit of considering all of them in prayer.

April 18: There comes a time in life when only wordlessness is an adequate language for prayer. Sometimes it comes in the middle of pregnancy. Sometimes it comes at the nursery window. Sometimes it shows itself in the middle of a raging storm. Sometimes it lurks within us certain but unidentified. Then we melt into a consciousness of God.

April 19: "Pray to God, but continue to row to the shore," the Russian proverb teaches. Dependence on God is not a substitute for doing God's will to the utmost ourselves. We can pray for peace, for instance, but unless we ourselves do something to bring it, it is an empty prayer, a kind of spiritual blasphemy.

April 20: Prayer turns a hunger for the goodness that is God into words.

April 21: When we have prayed prayers long enough, all the words drop away and we begin to live in the presence of God. Then prayer is finally real.

April 22: Reminder in a church bulletin: "Let us remember in prayer the many who are sick of our church and community." It's hard to know who to pray for in a situation like that. It must be tough for God, too.

April 23: "I have lived to thank God that all my prayers have not been answered," Jean Ingelow wrote. I am completely convinced, having lived through it so often in my own life, that when what we want most we do not get, we have not been deprived; we have been saved so that we could create the life we are really meant to have.

April 24: *The Book of Common Prayer* reads, "With the help of my God, I shall leap over the wall." The important thing to remember is that it is we who are supposed to do the leaping. God stands by.

April 25: The Talmud reads, "Never pray in a room without windows." Never pray without the world in mind, in other words. The purpose of the spiritual life is not to save us from reality. It is to enable us to go on co-creating it.

April 26: Every time we pray we come one step closer, not to changing God, but to converting ourselves.

April 27: "The higher goal of spiritual living," Rabbi Abraham Heschel taught, "is not to amass a wealth of information, but to face sacred moments." Prayer gives us the insights we need into the nature and purpose of life.

April 28: Unless we reflect always on the meaning of every moment in life, until we search long enough to find its place in the order of our private little universe, we will never find ourselves.

April 29: When we find ourselves simply sinking into the world around us with a sense of purpose, an inner light, and deep and total trust that whatever happens is right for us, then we have become prayer.

April 30: When we kneel down, we admit the magnitude of God in the universe and our own smallness in the face of it. When we stand with hands raised, we recognize the presence of God in life and our own inner glory because of it.

MAY

MATT. 10:16, 22

*I am sending you like sheep
among wolves. . . .
Everyone will hate you
because of me.
But whoever stands firm
until the end will be saved.*

*E*verything in life has something to teach us, if we only allow ourselves to look at it deeply enough. I don't talk about the incident much — for obvious reasons — but I don't forget it. (I mean, who can you talk to about what you learned from your dog?) His name was Danny. He was one of those wiry, intense, frenetic kind of Irish setters who go through life at high speed, laughing all the way. I have dozens of funny stories about him. Those are the ones I tell. There is one story, however, that is not funny at all. It comes back to me at strange times of life, at those moments when I am feeling most defensive and very vulnerable.

It was hunting season. The woods behind the monastery are thick, wide, and off-limits to hunters. Danny ran in those woods every day.

One afternoon he came back from a run, stood looking at me quiet as stone for a moment, and then lay down, stretched out the length of the throw rug in front of my desk, and looked at me lethargic and sloe-eyed. Something was wrong: no barking for the biscuit, no nudging my hands off the keyboard. Just the look. I got up from behind the desk, knelt down beside him, and ran my hands through the long scarlet feathering that covered his flanks and rib cage. When I felt it, he flinched only a hair and *then gave a deep, slow sigh. I parted the hair with both hands and saw the bullet hole in his ribs. There had been no sound, no agitation, no hysteria, no meanness. Just the trust that if he looked at me long enough, I would understand; if he waited long enough, it would be all right again.*

And it was, of course. The vet removed the bullet and, little by little, we loved him back to the same breathless energy and total irrepressibility he'd shown before the shooting. But I was never able to forget the incident as easily as he apparently had. I went on being troubled by the shooting, of course, but as the months went by, I found myself even more overwhelmed by the way the dog had responded to it. I got the distinct impression that it had been a good run in the woods and that it was worth it come what may.

The memory of the event touches my own life yet. I learned the power of vulnerability, of opening yourself to life, of entrusting yourself to other arms, come what may, and presuming that, in the end, it will all have been worth it. I learned from Danny that somehow, someway, if and when we are each cut down in the delirium of life, we will have all the resources we need to carry us through.

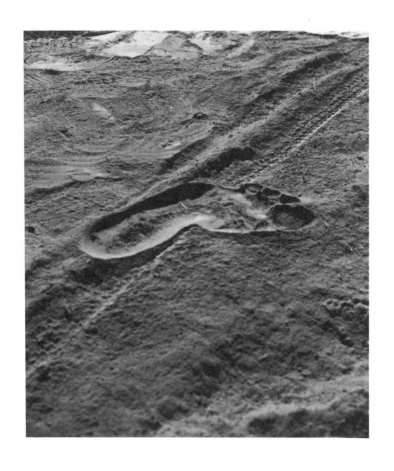

May 1: Survival is a by-product of trust. When we flail our way through life, the effort of it gets to be too much for us. It's learning to rest in the arms of the Creator that takes us through what could otherwise have destroyed us.

May 2: Vulnerability, the willingness to be taken out into the deserts of life, is not weakness. It is the ultimate in the virtue of hope.

May 3: When we open ourselves to the stranger, to the new experience, to the little things in life we've never tried before, we become new people. Why live in old skin forever, when God has given us the chance to know life on so many levels?

May 4: Life is a long walk through a fun house. Some of it seems very scary. Some of it is very funny. Some of it is very uncertain. But those who take every turn in the dark with a feeling of anticipation, who endure the best that life has to offer, are fully alive. It's when we hide in the corners of life, hands over our eyes, that we lose the price of admission.

May 5: Every act of conscience in life is an experience of being "a sheep among wolves." We have no idea what price we will pay for principle. We do know, however, that we will never be abandoned in it.

May 6: It's when we speak the truth in our hearts that we become real adults. That's when we become the fullness of ourselves and leave room for the voice of God in us.

May 7: Staying with a difficult situation to resolve it rather than trying to escape it gives God the chance to complete what such an experience was meant to effect in us.

May 8: We love the beaches and respect the mountains but fear the deserts of life. Yet, it is in the desert that we find out how strong we are and how beautiful is nothingness.

May 9: It isn't being able to control events to our advantage that really determines the value of our lives. It's being willing to work through the tough spots which, in the end, makes us everything we're able to be.

May 10: Until we have faced the controversies of life, explained our own position on them, and, at the same time, been open to the opinions, information, and attitudes of others, we have not really joined the human race. We have only been observers of the struggle rather than participants in the human quest for truth.

May 11: "Surviving means being born over and over," Erica Jong wrote. The point is that everything we survive in life provides us with one more layer of humanity with which to live it.

May 12: The scripture is clear: We are born to take a stand on behalf of the gospel, "to live like sheep among wolves." While we're busy saying private prayers it might not hurt to give some consideration to what our prayer life has enabled in us that makes the world a better place, a gospel place.

May 13: It isn't failure that destroys us. It's being afraid to fail that makes the next step in life impossible. But the willingness to fail and fail and fail again is what, in the end, leads to success. It's called "practice."

May 14: "Everyone will hate you because of me." Admit it: This is one gospel you and I want nothing to do with. After all, we're busy getting ahead.

May 15: "The best way out is always through," Robert Frost wrote. It's what we go through in life and finally best — or at least discover that it did not best us — that gives us quality, depth, and the ability to try again.

May 16: It is only when we ourselves have suffered that we can understand what it means.

May 17: We spend so much time trying to be tough that we miss the opportunity to be soft. We manage to hold the world at arm's length, but we fail to let in the very ideas, suggestions, insights that would make us more human, human beings.

May 18: Catherine of Siena taught: "Nothing great was ever done without much enduring." The trouble is that we are inclined to quit a thing too quickly. We quit when people tell us we'll never make it. We quit when we get tired. We quit when people don't approve. These criteria slow a lot of human progress. Worse than that, factors such as these limit our own development.

May 19: Strange, isn't it? What we want out of life is physical ease. What God wants of us is moral effort — not so much a narcissistic concentration on personal sin but a spiritual concentration on the building of a better world.

May 20: "If you wish to learn the highest truth," the Japanese proverb teaches, "you must begin with the alphabet." One thing in life builds on the other. Everybody knows that. The trick, of course, is summoning up the determination to start somewhere and burrow through to the end.

May 21: Maintaining a position that is out of step with society but perfectly in sync with the gospel is one of life's most difficult tasks. Name the position that is costing you most right now.

May 22: To prove our moral merit, we so often seek consolation in prayer when what we really need, if we are to come to moral maturity, is courage in the face of odds. It's funny how people want to talk about their prayer life when you begin to talk about the conditions around the globe. They seem to make a distinction between the two, but the truth is that the world may be the way it is because we choose prayer over the gospel. We want to make ourselves feel good when, if we were really people of prayer, we would be making the world feel good.

May 23: Each of us has a personal agenda — the thing we most want to do in life: feed the hungry, rescue the children, rebuild the city, reduce world conflict, eliminate nuclear weapons, achieve universal human rights for everyone — whatever their color, whatever their sexual orientation, whatever their gender. But when we let one good thing obliterate the others we are simply doing what has always been done: We are making a one-eyed world and calling it good.

May 24: Endurance is not a virtue when it tolerates evil.

May 25: "If we had been holier people," Templeton wrote, "we would have been angrier oftener." Which translated means: Never endure what is not in itself essentially good, or designed to make everybody's world a better place, or, in the end, really good for your own development. To violate any of those things is to violate the will of God for creation. God, scripture shows us, expects us to take a stand.

May 26: The things we endure are the things that define our own character.

May 27: When a fire broke out in his silos, the farmer called three fire companies. The first said it was much too large a fire for them to handle. The second said it was much too hot a fire for them to approach. Finally, he called a tiny little fire company and said, "If you'll just fight this fire, I'll give you $50,000!" He had hardly hung up when a little hook and ladder truck appeared at the top of the hill, lurched over the crest, raced faster and faster toward the blaze, and broke through the fire wall. Three men jumped out and began to spray water on the fire that surrounded them. Hours later they limped out of the smoking embers, wet, black, and exhausted. The farmer ran over to the chief: "I promised you I'd pay you and I will," he said. "What are you going to do with all this money, chief?" The fireman thought for a minute and then said, "Well, the first thing we're gonna do is get those lousy brakes fixed." Sometimes there's nothing to do but endure what we cannot avoid. The important thing is that we not give up. Whatever we survive well makes us even stronger than we were before it.

May 28: "An ox at the roadside, when it is dying of hunger and thirst, does not lie down," Olive Schreiner wrote. "It walks up and down — up and down, seeking it knows not what — but it does not lie down." I don't know enough about oxen to know if Schreiner is right, but one thing I'm sure about: When we quit in the midst of difficulty, we are certain to die. But if we keep trying to resolve the situation, we have at least a fifty-fifty chance of succeeding.

May 29: The gospel expects us to find ourselves under social pressure if we are really living what the gospel implies. So much for religion, the great spiritual massage. So much for the people who want prayer without contemplation, religion without reflection, and commitment without the courage to be what we say we believe in.

May 30: "When you put your hand to the plow," Alice Paul wrote in the midst of the struggle for woman's suffrage, "you can't put it down until you get to the end of the row." Until we learn to endure the pressures of the gospel, we can never really know its power.

May 31: "The difference between perseverance and obstinacy," Harriet Beecher Stowe wrote, "is that one comes from a strong will and the other one comes from a strong won't." Perseverance saves us because it enables us to try everything until something works.

Obstinacy destroys us because it refuses to imagine any way of doing a thing but ours. One opens us to the world; the other closes us off. Which approach is most like yours?

JUNE

MATT. 18:35

Forgive...from your heart.

The question is, What should we forgive and how do we do it? An ancient monastic story gives a flash of an answer, so subtle, so swift that its meaning is easy to miss. A young woman, the story tells, heavy with child and terrified of being executed for dishonoring the family name, accused a revered old monk, who prayed daily at the city gates, of assaulting her and fathering the child. The people confronted the old man with the accusation. But the old man's only response to the frenzy of the crowd was a laconic "Is that so?" as he gazed into space and went on fingering his beads. The townspeople, infuriated, drove the culprit out of town.

Years later, the woman, exhausted by her guilt and wanting to make restitution, finally admitted that it was her young lover, not the old monk at all, who was the father of the child. In fear for his life as well as her own, she had lied about the attack. Stricken with compunction, the townspeople rushed to the hermitage in the hills where the old man was still saying his prayers and leading his simple life. "The girl has admitted that you did not assault her," the people shouted. "What are you going to do about that?" But all the old monk answered was, "Is that so?" and went right on fingering his beads.

It's a disturbing story for those who want justice. It's an even more disturbing story for those who feel that they have not been given it. But I have come to believe the story has a great deal to tell us about forgiveness: What other people do to us may have little or nothing to do with forgiveness. The fact is that there is nothing to forgive in life if and when we manage to create an interior life that has more to do with what we are than with what other people do to us. What we are inside ourselves determines how we react to others — no matter what they do. What we cannot forgive is what we have not supplied for ourselves independent of the responses of those around us. We've all heard people say, "You can't hurt me." Often, we've even said it ourselves. The problem is that few of us mean it.

June 1: Once we know ourselves it is easy to forgive other people. The truth is that I am capable of everything they've ever done: Either I've never had the opportunity to do it or I've never been caught.

June 2: Forgiveness frees me from the burden of anger. What I refuse to forgive continues to harm me. It consumes my heart, poisons my mind, drains my energies, and cements my soul.

June 3: No matter how hurt I have been by someone I am far more than what they have taken away from me. Forgiveness that does not flow from this awareness is not forgiveness at all. Cheap forgiveness — forgiveness that is rushed in order to make everyone feel good — is a sad show that never ends, always returning to haunt us and only pretending at freedom. It is, therefore, at best, also useless.

June 4: Forgiveness occurs when we don't need to hold a grudge anymore, when we are strong enough to be independent of whatever, whoever it was that so ruthlessly uncovered the need in us. Forgiveness is not the problem; it's living till it comes that taxes all the strength we have.

June 5: The anger, the hurt, the bitterness that we carry from the past does little or nothing to harm the one who harmed us. It harms only ourselves. It is acid poured on our own souls, eating away at the peace in us.

June 6: Forgiveness is the gift that says two things: First, I am just as weak as everyone else in the human race and I know it. And second, my inner life is too rich to be destroyed by anything outside of it.

June 7: If you want to guard yourself against devastation, do what the teenage oracle says: "Get a life!"

June 8: Forgiveness and reconciliation are not the same thing. One enables us to move beyond the past. The other restores a relationship. The relationship is seldom as important as the restoration of inner peace that comes with recognizing that the past is past.

June 9: The inability to forgive another almost certainly arises out of an inability to forgive ourselves. When we refuse to give ourselves permission to be anything but perfect — as if failure did not bring its own lessons in life — we certainly are not able to forgive anyone else.

June 10: Some people think that forgiveness is incomplete until things are just as they were before. But the truth is that after great hurt, things are never what they were before: They can only be better or be nothing at all. Both of which are acceptable states of life.

June 11: Forgiveness is what we need when we think we don't and what we give when we think we shouldn't.

June 12: We know we have forgiven someone when we can meet that person with genuine acceptance in our hearts, wiser and warier than ever before, not of that person but of our own past expectations of the relationship.

June 13: What we carry in our hearts is what burdens our bodies.

June 14: "Our greatest glory," Confucius wrote, "is not in never falling but in rising every time we fall." War against the war within the self by making peace with it early. Yes, we have been hurt; no, we will never trust the same situation again. But indeed we will be happy always because we know more about life now than we did before and, when we are committed to going on, whatever the cost, we are more than capable of dealing with it.

June 15: We say, "Forgive and forget," but I think the saying is upside down. The real truth may well be that until we have forgotten why we were angry we haven't really forgiven the wrong. But the only way to do that is to get intensely involved in something else.

June 16: Fill your heart with beauty and you will find it increasingly difficult to waste your time on any kind of ugliness.

June 17: If forgiveness has something to do with forgetting, pray that God is an amnesiac. It seems impossible to hope from God what we withhold ourselves.

June 18: If the message we're supposed to be getting is really "Forgive us . . . as we forgive," it's time to let everything to the mercy of God, to put down unholy righteousness, to purge ourselves of grudges, and to move where we're welcome, uncaring of where we're not.

June 19: The Spanish proverb reads: "If I die, I forgive you; if I recover, we shall see." Why are you laughing?

June 20: Hannah Arendt wrote: "Forgiveness is the key to action and freedom." Why stay back where it hurts? Why stay stuck in the swamp of bitterness? Let the end to God and go where life has new promise. That's where God is calling you, so why stay where the voice has gone silent?

June 21: To forgive someone is not to say that what that person did to you is all right. It simply says that what that person did to you cannot, in the end, destroy you.

June 22: "Without forgiveness," Robert Assagioli wrote, "life is governed by an endless cycle of resentment and retaliation." What a waste of time. What a loss of perspective. What a diminishment of vision. What a poor investment of a life.

June 23: It takes no strength at all to require restitution. What takes strength is to be full enough of other things to be able to forego it.

June 24: "Life is an adventure in forgiveness," Norman Cousins said. You will, in other words, have lots of opportunity to practice. Don't wait too long to start, or life will have gone by before you ever lived it.

June 25: To withhold forgiveness is the adoration of the past, when it is the present that demands the best of us.

June 26: Mary Lou Kownacki writes, "There isn't anyone you couldn't love once you've heard their story." You know yours and how it affects you. Have you ever bothered to hear anyone else's?

June 27: It's one thing to "forgive" for the sake of civility. It is another thing to forgive "from the heart." Civility urges us to maintain the connections we have for the sake of our own advantage. The heart urges us to go beyond the hurt to the place where freedom lies and learning happens and trust is possible again, even if not here, not this.

June 28: Forgiveness does not ignore responsibility, but it does not tolerate vengeance. To jail criminals for life in order to protect the public is one thing; to become killers in order to punish them is vengeance.

Where does that fit in a divine schema that says, "Vengeance is mine; I will repay."

June 29: Beware of premature forgiveness: the kind that absolves another person without taking the time, making the effort to examine what the bitterness is saying to our own souls about our own needs and expectations.

June 30: A preacher stood over the bed of a dying man shouting, "Renounce Satan; renounce Satan and be forgiven!" The dying man opened one eye, looked at the preacher and said, "Sure, easy for you to say, Pastor, but in my situation I don't dare alienate anybody." The old man may have a point: You have to wonder if forgiveness that comes with strings attached is really forgiveness at all. If we forgive those who disturb us only on the condition that they give up other choices or freedoms or alternatives in life to suit our own agendas, have we really forgiven them at all? Or have we simply exercised our anger at them in a new way?

JULY

LUKE 17:16–19

Only a Samaritan returned to thank him. . . .
Your faith has made you well.

*T*ry replacing the word "Samaritan" in this month's quotation with something else, something closer to home. As in, "Only the man with the black leather jacket and the tattoos returned to thank him." Or, "Only the smelly old woman in the dirty dress returned to thank him." Or, "Only the gay couple from San Francisco returned to thank him." Or, "Only the foul-mouthed teenage girl returned to thank him." Get it? That's what this scripture is really all about. Life is full of surprises, all of them holy if we are holy enough to receive them.

For me, the lesson came home with greatest clarity in a strange country some years ago. I had become separated from my group in a cramped, sinuous, crowded bazaar on one side of a huge, dirty city in the Middle East. I was now a woman alone, surrounded by leering, staring men for whom a woman alone was easy prey. I had no idea whatsoever of where to go — just exactly what all the guides said must never happen. I elbowed my way up an incline out of the dark passages that separated the tiny boutiques, fighting panic with anger. At the top of the rutted path, I circled the mosque, heart pounding, looking for the cab and driver we'd engaged for the day, my only security. The dirt streets were a jungle of cars parked helter-skelter, bumper-to-bumper, with no common direc-

tion, no sense of order. The hot sun was finally cooling down for the day, but on the other side of it was night. I recognized nothing and no one. I couldn't read store signs. I couldn't use a telephone book to call a cab. I couldn't speak a single word of Arabic to ask for directions. I was at the mercy of a hostile environment. Suddenly a man, toothless, ragged, and dirty began screaming at me, jabbing at the air in my direction, running toward me on a stiff and twisted leg.

I was trapped in a sea of scrambled cars with my back to the wall of the mosque and my legs gone to pulp. He was lurching around cars, over hoods, trying to get at me. I began running wildly in the opposite direction. Suddenly, a young boy began chasing me, too. "No, no, lady. Stop," he shouted as he grabbed me. "It is all right. He is only trying to tell you that your taxi is over there on the other side." I blushed a deep, hot blush, ashamed to look at the crumpled old man who had finally caught up with me, gasping for breath and totally frustrated.

I learned something about the Samaritans of the world that day.

Scripture is teaching us not to count anybody out. Scripture is telling us to be open to surprise. Scripture is telling us that every person we meet is a potential source of life for us if there is only enough heart in us to accept it.

July 1: Everyone we meet in life is on a mission to teach us something new. Surprise!

July 2: Life is often where we least expect to find it. The dullest points of life may be exactly where God waits in disguise. Too bad we so seldom look there, isn't it?

July 3: When we begin by closing our minds to a thing, we make our own darkness of soul where light should be.

July 4: Don't be surprised by surprise; it's a regular part of life. The only problem is that we are more inclined to call the unexpected a "mistake" rather than a surprise. As a result, we evaluate things negatively before we even think of giving them a chance.

July 5: Surprise enables us to quit being in charge of the world for a while in order to enable the world to take us where our hearts have never been. It's only when we insist on being in control of everything that we shut ourselves off from new ways of being alive.

July 6: There's a Samaritan waiting in every one of our lives, the scripture implies: someone from whom we expect very little but from whom, if we listen, we can receive a great deal. Think a minute. Who was your Samaritan this week? Who surprised you with kindness or gratitude or insight?

July 7: Gratitude is the art of recognizing the debt we owe to others. Some of the people to whom we are most indebted are dead: Mozart, Hildegard of Bingen, Michelangelo. I always wonder if anyone ever told them how important their flashes of beauty were to the rest of the world, to our own souls. Then I wonder who I, myself, am overlooking, taking for granted today.

July 8: When surprise comes into a life it comes on horseback blowing a trumpet. And it scares us to death. The trick to surviving surprise is to learn to wait for it — smiling. Don't worry. It will come and it will be good for you.

July 9: Surprise is God's way of saying "hello." The response is optional.

July 10: John Donne says, "Those that see God see everything else." I say: Those that learn to see everything else learn to see God. When we fail to embrace the surprises in our lives, we miss the hidden side of the face of God.

July 11: "One can never pay in gratitude," Anne Morrow Lindbergh wrote. "One can only pay 'in kind' somewhere else in life." The purpose of blessing in life is to teach us to pass it on. The unspoken question of the parable of the healing is this: After Jesus healed him, whom did the Samaritan heal?

July 12: The Samaritan was healed because he believed that what he did not understand could be good for him. How quaint. How unusual. How wonderful. Such an attitude is the atrium to a whole new attitude toward life, the notion that the unexpected is expecting us everywhere.

July 13: I know a Samaritan when I see one: They're the people whose face I cannot read, whose background I do not know, whose reputation I do not like, and whose heart is unknown to me.

July 14: We never know where the good we do will come to fruit. The important thing is simply to keep on doing it in strange places in uncertain ways so that the heart we know least can be gifted, whether we know it happened or not.

July 15: Think of the people who did not come back to thank Jesus for healing them. We always assume that they were simply unappreciative or insensitive or ungracious. But I can't help but wonder if they really recognized the gift. It's possible, after all, to see and still be blind.

July 16: Don't be afraid to be afraid of something. It's when we want total control of a situation that we run the risk of losing the value of its surprise for us.

July 17: To live a life without a sense of surprise reduces us to the level of a robot: smart but not intelligent. We know what's going on; we just don't know what great gift it is for us.

July 18: To get a long stop light in the middle of traffic is the kind of surprise that nobody wants. Yet, it may be the only moment of the entire day when we really don't have to do a thing but be. What a pity to lose the opportunity.

July 19: The terrible thing about surprises is that you can't prepare for them. The nice thing about surprises is that, unprepared for them, we can try out new responses to life. We can say, "Oh, really?" instead of "Oh, no." We can open our hearts and let life in newly.

July 20: The purpose of surprise is to give us the chance to rethink first impressions, re-create old ideas, and renew a well-worn faith.

July 21: A naval officer stationed in the South Pacific for sixteen months got the following report from his wife about the petition their four-year-old had just added to her night prayers: "Dear God, please send me a baby brother so we'll have something to surprise Daddy with when he gets home." Surprise and shock are often the same thing. Don't worry; they both take us to new heights and new depths in life.

July 22: The nice thing about surprise is that you don't know it's coming so you can't make a mistake and refuse it. The only choice we have in the matter is the way we respond to it.

July 23: Samaritans, people who surprise us by breaking through our stereotypes, are interesting people: They require us to rethink everything we once thought we were certain about.

July 24: Surprise clears our heads of old certainties. It's the delete button of life. It prepares us to start life over again just when we were ready to settle down enslaved to our past understandings, our old despair.

July 25: Don't think for a moment that life is meant to proceed at a steady pace, in a regular form, with a standard structure, by a steady process. No, life is meant to lurch and limp along, full of surprises enough to keep us aware of it.

July 26: When the Samaritan returned to thank him, Jesus took hope. Maybe these people were redeemable after all. Maybe if he waited long enough, human beings would finally become fully human. In a nuclear world, a polluted world, a sexist world, we are still waiting. But, the scripture implies, don't give up: After all, the Samaritan did return. What more of a surprise can we hope for than that when all the good we ourselves do seems to fail.

July 27: Surprise works when, after it, we are different than we were before.

July 28: The fact that only the Samaritan thanks Jesus for the cure doesn't mean that the others in the group weren't grateful to have been healed. On the contrary. Most people are appreciative of the good things done to them. The surprise comes when they come back to say so. The fact is that we take blessings for granted. It's problems we talk about.

July 29: The nice thing about surprises is that they make us look at the rest of life differently, never knowing when something will happen to make it interesting again.

July 30: Think of it this way: Today is a surprise. Now, ask yourself this: Have you returned to say thanks for it yet? That's what I thought.

July 31: Samaritans are people who remind us to be what we insist we should be but seldom are. They startle us with a glimpse of our better selves just when we have almost forgotten the sight of it.

AUGUST

LUKE 14:34

Salt is good,
but if salt loses its taste,
how can it be restored?

Dreams drive us and disillusionment sobers us. Both of them are necessary parts of life.

When I look back now the story seems incredible — even to me. I was about nine years old. Somehow, somewhere I had come across one of those women's magazines that carried large ads full of mothers in aprons holding cans of scouring cleanser or with small children in sandboxes. It was Easter time, and this issue was different.

There on facing pages, in full color and stretching off every edge of the paper, was the picture of a blond, blue-eyed, curly-haired girl about my own age holding up a basket full of eggs and smiling out at me. She was wearing a flowing purple coat and purple shoes. Her large-brimmed straw hat was crowned with a thick purple ribbon, the tails of which fell across her shoulder and down the front of the coat. There was a small corsage of wild flowers on her lapel. Nothing had ever attracted my attention like that. I wanted it. All of it. I went around for days dreaming of how I'd look in that coat.

My mother, I remember, shook her head with the kind of dubious nod that mothers have. "It won't look good on you, Joan," she said, holding the page out at arm's length. "It's the wrong color for you. And you don't like hats."

She had something blue and tailored in mind, I think, but struck by the fact that I had finally shown interest in something besides a Nancy Drew mystery or a book about dogs and horses, she let the drama play itself out on its own terms.

The week before Easter when the stores were in a shopping frenzy, we walked the streets of the town for hours, from one store to another, one clothing department to another. I looked everywhere for purple coats that were not there, and then, reluctantly, I tried on the style and colors she clearly preferred. Finally, after hours of trying coats and discarding them, a determined little pout on my face, I found it in the most expensive boutique in town. There it was on a mannequin at the back of the store. The purple coat. The large-brimmed hat. I can feel the excitement, the triumph, in me even at the retelling of it. At last. I raced for the full-length mirror in the store front.

But something was wrong. Looking back at me in the mirror was someone I had never seen before. The full coat hung like a large, shapeless tent. The raglan sleeves drooped around my elbows. The collar sagged open. The purple was dull, not bright. The hat sat awkwardly on my head like a donut. And, worst of all, I wasn't blond. This was not the ad I had seen; it was not the dream I had dreamed at all. It was the brown, sour taste that comes with disillusionment, with the discovery that what you once called perfect is not.

It was, on the other hand, a very healthy disillusion-
ment. At the age of nine I learned that what we think we
want may be the last thing in the world we should really
have. I draped the coat around the mannequin again and
we left the store — I trying to dream another dream, my
mother smiling just a little.

Years later I got the purple cape I was really wait-
ing for.

August 1: What we dream about we will surely get — or at least some pale facsimile of it. What is important is not getting the dream but being able to appraise it once it's within reach.

August 2: Not to have a dream for tomorrow, for next year, for life is to abandon myself not simply to chance but to life without a rudder.

August 3: Dreams give us a destination toward which to steer, a reason to press forward when forward is impossible. Dreams promise a prize if we stretch ourselves beyond the humdrum of the present. A person without a dream is a person without a soul.

August 4: "Those who lose dreaming are lost," the Aboriginal proverb says. It's what we can imagine beyond the present that makes the future possible and the present bearable.

August 5: Beware the person who is too willing to accept the status quo in anything. Those types cut off blood to the heart.

August 6: The trick is to be able to follow a dream without becoming a captive of it — just in case what we think we want turns out to be the most artful of mirages.

August 7: What we are inclined to call in our realistic old age "the dreams of youth" may be the saddest commentary a person can make on the state of the human soul. Dreams don't die in youth; they are simply abandoned there for the sake of a deceit called "realism."

August 8: If the flavoring loses its flavor, the scripture asks, what can possibly flavor it? The question is not an idle one. What flavors the flavorings of my life is a serious question. The point is that the energy, the interests, the hopes we have are really the things that make life worth living.

August 9: Disillusionment is so often an abdication of personal responsibility. We look to something or someone else to fulfill our own best hopes, and when they don't, we blame them for our own inability to make life happy for ourselves.

August 10: If we lose the love for life that comes out of dreaming it to new fullness over and over again, what will ever sustain us from one stage of it to the other? Dreams are not only for the young.

Dreams make every stage of life the great adventure it is meant to be.

August 11: We need to examine what we have in life that will last if and when everything else is taken away.

August 12: When we set our hearts on one thing and one thing only, we doom ourselves to live crippled lives in cages far too small to grow a heart.

August 13: What we long for is the measure of our souls.

August 14: "Hope," Marquis de Vauvenargues wrote, "is the one thing that disillusion respects." Disillusion can damp the fire in our souls only when we refuse to see beyond it.

August 15: The nice thing about a dream is that we never get exactly what we set out to achieve — which means that there are always things left over to pursue when the journey of life goes dark. There is always a reason to go on, either because we have what we want and should enjoy it or because we do not have it and should try again.

August 16: Disillusionment and disappointment are not the same thing. Disillusionment comes out of investing more of me in something than I should ever give away. Disappointment is only a temporary detour along the way.

August 17: The function of disillusionment is to make us reevaluate what is really worth pursuing in life.

August 18: Disillusionment is a very important thing. Until we find ourselves disillusioned, we are far too inclined to worship what is not God.

August 19: We make the dreams of our life out of one of two things: clay or clouds. Clay is the dream we shape out of the life we've been given. Cloud is the dream we fashion out of nothing, that goes nowhere, that substitutes wishing for wanting.

August 20: A dream is what gives us the energy to make any effort it will take to get us where we want to go.

August 21: To dream without being willing to do something ourselves to make the dream come true dooms us to a life that never comes to fruit.

August 22: "Never confuse a single defeat with a final defeat," F. Scott Fitzgerald wrote. When we stop pursuing a dream before realization of the dream is clearly impossible, we fail to pursue our own best development. Then we have to ask what it is that is really blocking us: fear, insecurity, lack of initiative, or lack of faith?

August 23: The problem with disillusionment is that it is so closely linked to depression. Having found that the one option our soul could imagine is impossible, we think nothing is possible. Blinded in the soul, we lose hope in the heart.

August 24: Disillusionment blesses us with new sight. It makes us reach inside ourselves again to resolve what we have yet to confront directly.

August 25: We become disillusioned when something that presents itself as morally superior to the rest of us shows an immoral, a power-hungry, a callous side masking as goodness. The salt loses its flavor, and we don't know what to do without it. The real question, of course, is why did we put our hopes in it in the first place?

August 26: Just because we lose at something is no excuse to quit. If we are about something worthwhile, it is simply the sign that we must begin again.

August 27: Rabindranath Tagore wrote: "The mountain remains unmoved at seeming defeat by the mist." Point: Failure is not necessarily failure at all. It may simply be part of the process of becoming what we are really meant to be. Until we know defeat, we are almost never capable of real success.

August 28: The kinds of dreams we have determine the quality of our lives. The problem is not that we don't dream. The problem is that we seldom dream high enough.

August 29: Show me a dreamer and I'll show you one of God's heartbeats for the human race.

August 30: There's a great difference between a plan and a dream. A plan specifies the steps we're supposed to take to get where we already know we're going. A dream charts a direction to a place we are willing to make exist.

August 31: "Of course, there's a Santa Claus, Virginia," the father said to his clearly skeptical but still dreamy-eyed child. "That was Santa Claus at Rocke-feller Center; that was Santa Claus at Macy's; and this is Santa Claus right here on this street corner." The little girl, growing more disillusioned by the minute, said, "But how can there be so many Santa Clauses?" So the father turned to the fellow in the big red suit and said, "Go ahead, Santa. Tell Virginia how you fell into the Xerox machine." Point: Disillusionment is the bridge to reality.

SEPTEMBER

MARK 4:38

Master,
does it not concern you
that we are going to drown?

An *African woman told me recently, with apology and dismay, "Sometimes we wonder if whites are completely human." Her voice was soft and there was real pain, real uncertainty in her eyes. I understood why. I had seen the miserable places where in an apartheid system 20 percent of the population, white, had confined 80 percent of the population — black and without homes, without electricity, without water — to "locations," to "homelands," to "settlements." Then I thought of segregation in the United States, the extermination of women and children, old and young, in Hiroshima and Nagasaki, the carpet bombing of Dresden, the slaughter of Indians, the lynching of blacks, the rape hotels in Bosnia — and the firebomb deaths of three little boys in Ireland recently because one parent was Protestant, one Catholic. I thought of everything humans have done to one another throughout history. And I understood the question. I understood the dismay, the despair that comes from suffering. As a result, I also understood this month's scripture passage a little better. It raises no small spiritual question: "Does God care," the suffering ask, "if we are drowning?" Does God care when we have our face in the dust, a boot on our back, a hole in our heart from the loss of a job, the death of someone we love, the collapse of a great project, the humiliation of failure, the indignity of oppression?*

Apparently not. Yet, if we look around at what God has provided for our lives — the beauty, the food, the people, the music, the land — the answer must surely be yes. God cared enough to give us life; God surely cares that we be able to live it well. But if that's the case, we can't blame God for what we do to hurt either ourselves or one another. Maybe the real question ought to be, "Do we ourselves care enough to do something about it? Are any of us really human enough yet to do something to stop all the pain?"

One thing for sure, when we cannot escape pain, the way we handle it is saying something to us about the quality of our own souls, the development of our own spirits.

September 1: When the storms of life assail us our first temptation is to quit it, to be delivered from "this vale of tears." We have no time for darkness, no love for doubt. We want to live unlimited by anything. But limitation may be the very thing that leads us to create our new and better selves.

September 2: "Holy One," the disciple said, "how many people have you cured?" "Oh, almost none," the Holy One said. "But that can't be true," the disciple protested. "People come to you from everywhere." "Ah, that's true," the Holy One said, "but most people don't come to be cured. They come to feel better. If they really wanted to be cured, they would have to change." Most of the storms of life we could calm easily — if we ever really did something to change ourselves in the situation.

September 3: "We are all born mad," Samuel Beckett wrote. "Some remain so." So often, like children, we demand more of life than life can give. That in itself is the kind of madness that makes our suffering for ourselves.

September 4: When our expectations continue to exceed our reality, to the point where our lives are miserable because of it, we can be sure that we have not outgrown the madness of our spiritual adolescence. We have not yet grown to the point of mental maturity where we can work for change but live in peace until it comes.

September 5: When we think that God is asleep in our lives, that may be the very moment that God is being most active, but we are too asleep to notice.

September 6: There is a difference between depression and despair. Depression is when we know that however bad life may be at least God alone surely cares. Despair is when we begin to think that what we see around us is all that God ever intended life to be.

September 7: Loss can so often be the first step to something better — either around us or within us.

September 8: Whatever it is that bothers us is the sign of what we should be doing in life. When we find ourselves in the midst of a storm, it is time to change something.

September 9: Adversity is God's way of making us look for what is really important, really gift, in life.

September 10: The storms of life are what lead us to look for help. That's not weakness; that's simply the admission that being human requires us to be connected to the rest of the human race.

September 11: Never fail to ask for help when you need it. Those who swallow a stone become a stone. When we insist on denying our needs we deny our own humanity to such a point that one day we wake up and we're not really human anymore. We are simply lumps of stone where warmth and joy and growth should be.

September 12: Sometimes we look for God only when we are in the midst of one of life's great storms. In that case, blessed be life's great storms.

September 13: Once we have survived one of the great storms of life, we come to realize that we can survive all of them — not because God intervened to save us but because God gave us the strength to save ourselves.

September 14: There is a moment in every life where it seems that our present suffering, whatever it is, will never end. Then, all we can rely on is the fact that God is in it with us.

September 15: We so often forget that the beauty of the story of the storm in scripture is not so much that in the end Jesus calmed it but that Jesus stood by while it was happening. The message is clear: We can endure anything when we know that we have the strength within ourselves to withstand it.

September 16: It is not suffering that is the end of the world for us; it is despair that destroys us.

September 17: Triumph is not what makes us great; it is the ability to withstand failure that is the mark of faith. "To be vanquished and yet not surrender, that is victory," Josef Pilsudski wrote.

September 18: We fear struggle and we discount failure, but in the end it may only be struggle and failure that make us what we are.

September 19: Jesus did not eliminate the storm; he simply saved the people on board the sinking ship from giving in to it.

September 20: "Doubt whom you will, but never yourself," Christian Bovee wrote. We must know that we can survive whatever life deals us or we will never survive anything.

September 21: The fear of life is what destroys life. What is there from which we cannot learn how to be stronger tomorrow?

September 22: When we cease to realize that storms are part of life, not interruptions of life, we can live from one to the other with real equanimity, growing stronger all the time. How much better to die whole than only half-developed.

September 23: No healthy person seeks suffering, but only healthy people survive it well.

September 24: God calms our storms when we get strong enough to endure them. Maybe the disciples in the storm were really only meant to learn how to go on hanging on to the boat when hanging on seemed impossible.

September 25: There are times in life when the felt absence of God seems almost impossible to bear. The temptation is to lose faith. But it is at those very moments that we need to look for God in other places than where we expected God to be. It is a call to move on. The problem is that we want God to be where God is not instead of looking for life in another place.

September 26: When God seems most indifferent to us may be the very moment when God is calling us most clearly to something else.

September 27: God always cares for us, but God does not always care for us the way we want to be cared for at the time. And, in the end, we may discover that that was the greatest caring of them all.

September 28: We fear the storms of life, but we fail to realize the strength they create in us, the insight they develop in us, the call they are to us to make a better world.

September 29: I don't believe that God wants us to "offer pain up." I believe that God wants us to brave it — and change it.

September 30: We must not make God an excuse to bear the unbearable. We must bear what we cannot change, of course, but we must also work to change what we cannot bear.

OCTOBER

MATT. 6:25

Do not be anxious about your life.

Everything in life teaches us something about what it is to be human until, if we are listening and learning all our lives, we ourselves become everything we can possibly be. We begin the search for fullness of life at a very early age. We choose heroes, icons of what we ourselves would like to become.

All the heroes of my early life were people of action. I valued explorers, presidents, civil rights activists, suffragettes, friends, and family members who were brave enough, decisive enough, strong enough to make things happen. It was only as I got older and people I loved began to die that I discovered the lesson, the courage of calm:

Uncle Lou faced cancer in the 1950s when it was the scourge of modern medicine, but he talked to me quietly and gently about my own future two days before he died.

Sister Theophane closed her eyes in the middle of pain, smiled, and slipped into a forty-day period of comatose waiting after a lifetime of competence and efficiency.

My mother, a brilliant woman, suffered the ravages of Alzheimer's disease for twenty-eight years and went from its early forms of agitation to a kind of distant inner existence untroubled by anybody or anything.

In each of those situations a kind of chaos infected the world. Yet, at the same time, each of them brought with it a new kind of insight. No doubt about it: The lesson I learned from death was the lesson of calm. After all, what use was flailing and raging when life went inevitably on? Or, as the case may be, would not go on at all.

The problem, of course, lies in learning to determine when calm is courageous and when chaos is holy. When is acceptance holy and chaos madness? When is chaos holy and acceptance weakness? Maybe we never know. But that's not important. What is important is to keep asking the question and to develop the ability to be both resolutely calm and courageously holy as the situation demands.

October 1: There is a kind of calm that is passive acceptance of the unacceptable. When the world around us is falling mercilessly on the backs of people who cannot bear the burden or did not cause the destruction, to be calm in the midst of evil is not good. Then we must do something. But calmly.

October 2: To spend life worrying about what we cannot control or do not know with certainty will happen makes a mockery of faith and a shell of hope.

October 3: "Never cut what you can untie," Joseph Joubert wrote. We rush where we could walk and we run where we do not need to go. And when we get there, there's nothing left inside of us to have bothered to bring.

October 4: What we do with too much haste we live to regret. What we do with reflection we can respect all our lives.

October 5: Life is not a Gordian knot; it is not a problem to be solved. Life is a process to be lived in the surety that, in the end, things will, if we allow them, come out just as they should.

October 6: Calm is a virtue only when it implies stability in the face of chaos, not when it is simply an excuse for refusing to act. That's not calm, that's "becalmed." There's not a sailor in the world who doesn't know the difference.

October 7: What is the use of being agitated? It serves only to irritate the spleen, not to resolve the problem.

October 8: There comes a moment in life when we finally realize that most of what we worry about is not worth the worry. Then the calm sets in, the synonym for which may well be maturity.

October 9: Apathy is not calm. To be resigned to what must be changed is simply complicity with evil.

October 10: When we understand the dimensions of a situation with all its dangers, all its risks, all its demands, calmness is the only thing that will keep us ready to face it, able to survive it, come what may.

October 11: Calm and resignation are not the same thing. Resignation is what's left when we don't stay calm enough to do the right thing in the first place.

October 12: "Calmness," Ralph Waldo Emerson wrote, "is always Godlike." If you are God, you know that life always goes "wrong." The question, of course, is: What is really "right"? Better to go through the process calmly till the storm ends and the skies are brighter than to fly into a panic and miss the new moment completely.

October 13: The old hymn reminds us, "Be still my soul" in times of distress. Then, and only then, when we stay still and listen, can we hear the voices of wisdom around us, both within and without.

October 14: The Irish have a phrase for it: They call hysteria "losing the run of yourself." The implications of the statement are clear. When we lose our calm, we lose the best of ourselves to wild gesturings that lack both substance and direction.

October 15: Calmness is not an affectation of public propriety. It is a state of inner peace that is impervious to the winds of change around us.

October 16: The old "stiff upper lip" — the ability to pretend that nothing has affected us when something certainly has or certainly must — is a poor imitation of the calm that comes from believing that whatever we are forced to face in life can be dealt with without our being destroyed by it.

October 17: Never be afraid of chaos. It is simply order rearranging itself.

October 18: Chaos is the foundation of creativity. "The first act of creation," e. e. cummings says, "is destruction." Until one system falls, another can never rise. That's why saving a dying past only prolongs the inevitable.

October 19: "Adopt the pace of nature," Emerson writes. "Her secret is patience." We are not a patient people, we Americans. We believe more in the instant than in the coming. We make hysteria one of the hallmarks of effectiveness and, in the end, perhaps, mix results with effectiveness.

October 20: To be impatient is to miss a lot of beauty, to push a lot of children to become adults too quickly, to become a trade-in society with little or no respect for what, having served well in the past, still has value in the present. We so commonly overlook what only the heart, calm enough to trust the present, can really see.

October 21: Driven by a need for results, we miss the sight of trees growing and flowers opening and relationships becoming. We push and prod and commit ourselves to a kind of "progress" that misses a lot of life because we are not calm enough to let a thing develop through every necessary stage from slim beginning to satisfying end.

October 22: Why go through a thing calmly when you can wear yourself out before the project even begins by going into a panic about it? Then it won't really make any difference whether it succeeds or not. You will have already endured the worst. That's called the storm before the calm.

October 23: "Why are you crying?" the teacher asked the child. "Are your parents mean to you?" "No," the child said. "My parents are the kindest people in the world?" "Do they neglect you?" the teacher said. "No, they don't," the child said. "They play with me and tell me stories every night." "Do they refuse to get you what you want?" "No," the little boy went on sobbing. "They get me the best of everything." "Then why in heaven's name are you crying?" the teacher asked again. "Because I'm afraid they might try to run away." Ah, why enjoy what is when you can worry about what might be coming?

October 24: There is a kind of chaos that releases possibility. Most people fear an environment that encourages new ideas. They prefer what is because they fear what might be if they're not in control of it.

October 25: The colors we paint our rooms, the types of music to which we choose to listen, the volume at which we play the TV, the degree of clutter in a room all contribute to the mental state through which we view our world.

October 26: If you feel anxious all the time, it might be time to clean out the cupboards, empty the desk drawers, change the flowered wallpaper, and sit down somewhere alone. It's amazing how silence changes the face of chaos and raises the level of calm in the world.

October 27: Road rage is nothing but the loss of personal calm let loose upon the world at large.

October 28: When calm is impossible and chaos is the order of the day, try to remember that God created the world out of nothing and, God willing, if we stay at this thing long enough, something may come out of this mess, too. Or as Ella Wheeler Wilcox put it: "The splendid discontent of God with chaos made the world."

October 29: "Concern should drive us into action," Karen Horney wrote, "not into depression." There is no virtue in complaining about things we refuse to do something to improve, to change, to open to public examination. That kind of calm only increases the problem.

October 30: Pace has become a synonym for progress. As a result we find ourselves rushing from one thing to another, hectic and exhausted, when learning to savor life, to milk the moment has become the lost art of human development. We must learn to cultivate what Adrian Cowell calls "the slow rhythm of waiting."

October 31: People who are really interested in raising the level of calm in a discussion and slowing the pace of the world start by lowering the level of their voices and slowing the speed of their talk.

NOVEMBER

LUKE 12:35

*Be dressed for service and
have your lamps burning ready.*

I*t was Christmas Day, an unlikely time, when it happened. He was driving across town from his brother's
home to ours for Christmas dinner. The ice storm that
came up suddenly during the day left the streets empty
and slick. Every road was a rink of danger. Dad's car
spun on an empty street, jumped a curb, cracked a telephone pole, and came to a befuddled stop, askew and
confounded but not really very damaged, not smashed
and crashed and crumpled. It was, at most, to the ca-
sual bystander, a kind of comic scene: Charlie Chaplin
doing a harmless pratfall. And yet Dad died in that moment's slippage. Life went and lives changed. We were
not prepared.*

*But as the years went by, I began to understand that
"preparation" is more hope than reality. Who is ever really
prepared for anything life-altering — the lost loved one,
the lost job, the lost home, the lost future — even when
we think we're prepared? And how is it even possible for
us to prepare for such a thing even if we want to, even if
we tell ourselves every day of our lives that we must "be
prepared"?*

*The answer may well be that perhaps we can't. Perhaps
we're not even supposed to be prepared. Perhaps we are
only supposed to be ready to lose. Perhaps the truth is that*

we are only to be ready to accept the role and place of grief in life. Why? Because grief is that slice of life that takes us beyond the boundaries of our mind and makes us see life anew again. It is possible that when life is just the way we like it, life is far, far too small to do what life is really meant to do.

November 1: Grief grows us up. When we come to understand that whatever we have we can lose, we begin, first, to hold everything lightly and, second, we learn to squeeze happiness dry.

November 2: Grief is the sign that we loved something more than ourselves.

November 3: Grief makes us worthy to suffer with the rest of the world.

November 4: Suspect "the stiff upper lip" philosophy of grief. It is meant for the comfort of those who do not grieve, not for the relief of those who do. We are a people who are very disquieted by someone else's sorrow.

November 5: Don't be afraid to grieve your losses. They are the signposts of our lives, after which we are never the same again.

November 6: Grief destroys us only when we deny it or ignore it. In those cases we refuse to deal with what we've lost so we have no idea what we need to do in its wake. Then the pain can become so permanent we don't even know we have it.

November 7: The little losses of life prepare us to survive the great ones. We find out little by little as we go through one small change after another that it is possible after loss — no matter how bottomless the pit initially — to laugh again, to love again, to begin again. Practice savoring your little losses. They may be what saves you in the end.

November 8: Grief is a process of many stages and no guaranteed cutoff points. When something happens that in our minds should not have happened — the child dies, the group betrays us, the loved one leaves, the world is wracked with disaster — there is no charting the time it will take to recover. There is only the sure knowledge that we can recover if for no other reason than that so many have. And, astoundingly, often even better than before.

November 9: The first stage of grief is disbelief. We refuse to accept the fact that something devastatingly final has erupted into the middle of our lives. Our minds know that now there is no going back, but our hearts stay locked in the past. This is the stage that melts the soul of certainties.

November 10: The second stage of grief is when we believe the loss to be unbearable and so we go numb. We refuse to feel what we fear we cannot endure. And in that refusal we run the risk of becoming numb to everything. This is the stage that saves us from desolation but dims our vision.

November 11: The third stage of grief is when we begin again to believe enough in ourselves to be able finally to let go of one stage of life in order to embrace the rest of it once more. This is the stage that resurrects the heart.

November 12: Grief is a process, not an event. As Emily Dickinson puts it:

After great pain, a formal feeling comes — ...
This is the Hour of Lead —
Remembered, if outlived,
As Freezing persons, recollect the Snow —
First — Chill — then Stupor — then the letting go — .

November 13: "Life," Djuna Barnes says, "is the permission to know death." Once we realize that everything we touch is in the act of disappearing we shall touch it more intensely. The very thought of grief prepares us to live well.

November 14: Life and death are not separate parts of life. They are life lived to the hilt. One comes from nothing; the other goes to nothing. To be really alive is to have the courage to trust both parts of the process, to know that each is a preparation for the joy of the other.

November 15: Are you really afraid of death? Then ask yourself, could you really go on forever?

November 16: Grieve the loss of sight, yes, but remember that it may more than anything else open the vision of the soul.

November 17: Grieve the loss of taste, of course, but know that it may sharpen the sense of touch.

November 18: Grieve the loss of hearing, indeed, but know that it may bring the capacity for observation to fullness.

November 19: Grieve the loss of limbs, without doubt, but realize that physical impairment may bring us more to an awareness and appreciation of place than any other loss.

November 20: To tell those in grief not to grieve may be the unkindest cut of all. It denies them the right to reevaluate their lives, to treasure their past, and to be accompanied through their new fears. Because we are not prepared to deal with the reality of loss, we want no one else to face it either.

November 21: Learn from the grief of those who, after great loss, live in regret, with a sense of guilt for what they did not do before. Accept the fact that what you are doing today you are doing because it serves your present purpose. Admit to yourself why you are doing what you are doing. Take responsibility for that now. Perhaps what you are doing now is not ideal, but at least you will not wonder in the future why you did it.

November 22: Be grateful for grief. It is an infallible sign that we have loved something deeply enough to miss it.

November 23: We know the value of ritualizing grief, but we do not always appreciate the value of expressing it for fear that admitting it could become a need to wallow in it. We confuse the two. Grief is the necessary act of expelling the long, low wail of desolation that fills every pore in the body. The heart never seeks unhappiness. When the heart has exhausted its pain, the heart begins to beat again.

November 24: "Wallowing" is the act of overreacting to something that has long since lost the power to affect a person so keenly. People grieve for the part of them that has been lost and then brighten when life takes its new shape. Grief runs a course. Wallowing can go on forever because, for some reason we ought to examine, we refuse to admit when it's over.

November 25: Grief and depression are not the same thing. Grief is an immediate response to an immediate loss that is very depressing, perhaps, but not without situational resolution. What one circumstance creates, another can cure: I lose one husband and am very unhappy but marry another and am overjoyed again. Depression, on the other hand, is a shapeless sense of malfunction often unknown, commonly unnamed. Grief, in other words, is not a terminal disease. It is the door to another life just waiting to be opened.

November 26: Grief is the gift of memory. Rita Mae Brown says, "I still miss those I loved who are no longer with me but I find I am grateful for having loved them. The gratitude has finally conquered the loss."

November 27: "The perpetual work of your life," Michel de Montaigne wrote, "is but to lay the foundation of death." All of life is a preparation for what we shall become. The only question is whether what we do is really what we want to be. And if not, why are we doing it?

November 28: The things we lose in life all teach us something. They prepare us to choose more profoundly the next time.

November 29: Think of it this way: "Grief at the absence of a loved one," Jean de La Bruyère says, "is happiness compared to life with a person one hates."

November 30: Lucy says it all the time: "Good grief, Charlie Brown." Now what do you suppose that means? Maybe it means that those with lamps burning are prepared for anything — even grief — and that's the real good in life.

DECEMBER

JOHN 1:23

I am, as Isaiah prophesied,
the voice of one crying out
in the wilderness,
"Make straight the way of God."

I t was not what I expected to have happen at a White House Conference in Washington, D.C., on the relationship of the faith community to race relations in the United States. But because of that meeting I began to realize what Christmas is really all about. We were black, white, and brown, Muslims, Hindus, Christians, Baha'i, and Native Americans called together to discuss the relationship of religion to race. Ironically enough, it was the Indian chief who taught me the meaning of Isaiah.

Into the midst of the theological meanderings of those of us who wanted to write another paper, have another meeting, take another workshop to combat racism, the chief brought the message of Isaiah again. He stood up slowly, folded his hands quietly in front of him, looked out over our heads, and said softly, "I have spent my life teaching our children to say 'thank you': Thank you for the grass. Thank you for the rain. Thank you for the stranger. Thank you for all the people of the world. I think that if we learn to say 'thank you' for everything, we will come to realize its value, to respect it, to see it as sacred."

It was a simple speech, but it had a kind of cataclysmic effect on my soul. It gave me pause. It made me think. It raised the specter of Isaiah in me all over again. It made me think newly about what the scriptures are really *talking about when they tell us to "make straight the way of God." I suddenly realized that Christmas is time to shout "thank you."*

Christmas is the commitment to life made incarnate. It is the call to see God everywhere and especially in those places we would not expect to find glory and grace. It is the call to exult in life.

Christmas is the obligation to see that everything leads us directly to God, to realize that there is no one, nothing on earth that is not the way to God for me. I knew instantly that the moment we begin to really celebrate Christmas, to look at everyone and everything as a revelation of God, to say "thank you" for them, that racism would be over, war would be no more, world hunger would disappear, everything would be gift, everyone would be sacred.

Indeed, it is simple, but, oh, so clear: All we have to do to "make straight the way of God" is to say "thank you," to learn to live intensely, to have a zeal for life, to develop a passion for life.

December 1: This year when you open a gift at Christmastime, when you say "thank you," remember that this particular gift is only meant to be a reminder of the goodness of God calling you to be the voice crying in the wilderness that gives passionate thanks for everything, for everyone, in life.

December 2: We need a passion for life, a surge of gratitude, so deep that we will do whatever it takes to guarantee the fullness of life for the entire world.

December 3: The Koran teaches: "None of you will believe till you want for your brothers and sisters what you want for yourself." The call to humanity to have a passion for humanity is God's great call through every major religion, of course, but certainly through the Jesus who walks through life as a healing presence wherever he goes.

December 4: Whatever you do, do it with passion. Otherwise why do it at all?

December 5: When a sense of zeal leaves our life, it is time to begin again, because whatever we have been doing up to now has clearly died in us.

December 6: Passion is what is left over after mere duty is done. Passion is what wakes us up when we think we are too tired to go on.

December 7: "There's plenty of fire," Rachel Field wrote, "in the coldest flint." If we want to revive something within us, we must begin to give thanks for it again.

December 8: So many times in life we find ourselves merely going through the motions, doing things because we think we have to do them. And that's probably true. But it is just at those moments that we most need to develop some new outlets, plan some new experiences, and begin some new activities. Otherwise the weight of dry responsibilities may well damp the fires of the heart that we ourselves have allowed to die. When the fire of zeal goes out, the lamp of life goes out with it.

December 9: Christmas reminds us that God gives us one chance after another in life to become new again, to let things grow in us, to birth in ourselves fresh and different ways to God.

December 10: The saddest thing in life is to lose interest in it. When we can learn to say thank you for the hot coffee, thank you for the quiet, thank you for the children whose energy taxes our own, then we are on our way to tasting life, to wallowing in it, to letting it run down our faces into our mouths and, then, to laugh out loud about the whole thing.

December 11: A child in a manger is God's way of telling us that life is a process of eternal newness, unending openness, and passion without end.

December 12: The German philosopher Hegel wrote, "Nothing great in the world has been accomplished without passion." In fact, I am inclined to think that nothing normal has been either. It takes passion — commitment to something, love for something, devotion to something — just to turn the Mondays of life into periods of doable duty.

December 13: It is only the risk of enthusiasm that makes life livable. People who wait to be coaxed into life have really stopped living it years before for whatever the reason. "Convince me," "make me," "prove it" — people sit and wait for life to come to them. But the real trick to life is to make it out of nothing by the intensity we carry in our own hearts for it.

December 14: Whatever it is that stirs our souls is what measures the quality of our lives, makes a claim on our time, and fills our minds no matter what else we may seem to be doing.

December 15: To go through life without zeal for something is to go through life half-awake, half-engaged, half-alive. When we realize that, it's not really a problem. When we don't, it can be terminal.

December 16: The question passion asks of every human being is not, For what are you willing to die? That one would be easy. The real question passion asks of us is, For what are you willing to live? Beware any answer that sounds like "I don't know."

December 17: To be able to be exuberant about something is one of life's greatest gifts. Never take it for granted. Nurture it. Give in to it at all times, no matter who goes *tsk, tsk* behind you. Exuberance may be the only proof we have that we are really alive.

December 18: Exuberance is infectious. What excites you will eventually excite the rest of the world. We are all simply a microcosm of the world. Whatever you and I want we must ourselves become or how can it ever become real anywhere else?

December 19: The poet Edna St. Vincent Millay wrote what may be the irrefutable answer to people whose first thought is self-protection. Millay said,

> *My candle burns at both ends;*
> *It will not last the night;*
> *But, ah, my foes, and oh, my friends —*
> *It gives a lovely light!*

It is possible that the world has far too few of those who live like that.

December 20: Bethlehem and the manger were foolish. Nazareth and the carpentry were foolish. Galilee and the lepers were foolish. But the energy of them marked the world, gave it new vision, raised its hope. If we live without being foolish about something great we can, of course, live very comfortably. The question is, Will we have lived well?

December 21: Passion is not pallid and not dour. Passion is what gives meaning to what seems meaningless, energy to what seems impossible, direction to what is scattered. Without passion we only wander through life; we do not proceed with purpose. So how can we ever be sure that we got where God intended us to go?

December 22: The *Rule of Benedict*, an ancient document, warns against the pitfalls of "bitter zeal." There is, the Rule states, "A zeal that leads to life." And presumably, therefore, a zeal that leads to death. So how, in our intensity, do we tell the difference? Good zeal is the passionate pursuit of anything that leads to the good of the rest of the world, harms no one, and gives hope to many. It is a baby born in a manger who dies on a cross.

December 23: Thomas Fuller writes: "Zeal without knowledge is fire without light." It is not enough to be passionate about something. It is also necessary to understand it.

December 24: Zeal is not chauvinism; it is ardor. It is the kind of love that moves mountains to save a single soul.

December 25: The philosopher Kierkegaard wrote, "What our age lacks is not reflection but passion." We know a lot of things in this world now: How many poor children there are in the center of our cities, how many families lack insurance, lack health care, lack homes, how many people go to bed hungry at night. But where is the passion that turns the birth of Jesus into the life of Jesus?

December 26: When we really get passionate about something, someone will invariably tell us to "be reasonable," "stay cool," "calm down." It's such a clever way of controlling a person. The thing Isaiah wants us to learn is that we must never be cool, calm, or reasonable about the irrational. The manger reminds us that it is our responsibility to make God's will possible in life. Or as Henry S. Haskins says, "Good behavior is the last refuge of mediocrity."

December 27: Balzac says, "Passion is universal humanity. Without it religion, history, romance, and art would be useless." I say they would be impossible, nonexistent, invisible, too.

December 28: Don't be afraid of passion. It is passion that really drives us to make possible what would otherwise be completely impossible if we followed our minds instead of our feelings.

December 29: Thought changes nothing. Feeling does.

December 30: The wag put it this way: "We are all in the same boat with Christopher Columbus. He didn't know where he was going when he started. When he got there he didn't know where he was. And when he got back he didn't know where he'd been." So enjoy. Wherever you are, whatever is going on in your life right now is the birthing place of God for you. Say thank you.

December 31: We are at the beginning of a century in which the whole world is in a state of rebirth. Be passionate about God's will for every living thing: every wetland, every ocean, every child, every inner city, every woman, every moment of life. Live passionately. Live intensely. Live with enthusiasm. Make straight the way of God.

Welcome to . . .

The Monastic Way

by Joan D. Chittister, O.S.B.

If you are a seeker of the sacred . . .
If spirituality is an important part of your life . . .
If you would like a daily companion along the way . . .

Subscribe to . . .

The Monastic Way

This monthly, single-page publication with daily reflections by one of today's most inspiring religious writers and speakers is ideal for:

- Personal daily reflection
- Homily starters
- Opening prayers for classes, meetings, group gatherings
- Faith sharing

$15 per year includes postage; add $3 for overseas mailing.

Send to *Benetvision,* 355 E. Ninth St., Erie, PA 16503-1107
or call (814) 459-5994. Fax: (814) 459-8066

Quantity discounts available upon request.

ORDER FORM for The Monastic Way
Use this order form for your personal subscription or gift subscriptions.

Name of recipient _____

Address _____

City _____ State ____ ZIP_____

Phone (_____)_____

If gift, name of sender _____

❒ $15 is enclosed for each subscription ($12 subscription + $3 postage).
(Please add an extra $3.00 for overseas mailing.)

❒ Quantity discounts are available upon request.

Mail to: *Benetvision,* 355 East Ninth St., Erie, PA 16503-1107
Phone (814) 459-5994   Fax (814) 459-8066